By Edwin Woodgate
© Copyright 2014

Disney

"Where dreams come true"

Table of Contents

Introduction

Chapter 1: Early Childhood Years

Chapter 2: Walt Disney's Teenage Years

Chapter 3: The Kansas Years – 1920 – 1923

Chapter 4: The Hollywood Years – 1923 – 1928

Chapter 5: Walt Disney – The Family Man

Chapter 6: Silly Symphonies and Early Success in the 1930s

Chapter 7: More Early Success – 1929 – 1939

Chapter 8: Disney Brothers' Success and Failure – 1939 – 1941

Chapter 9: Walt Disney and World War II

Chapter 10: Disney Animation – Post World War II to 1955

Chapter 11: Walt Disney and the Planning of Disneyland

Chapter 12: The Opening of Disneyland and its Legacy

Chapter 13: Walt Disney – Film and Television Post 1955

Chapter 14: Walt Disney and the Planning of Disney World and EPCOT

Chapter 15: Walt Disney's Illness and Death

Chapter 16: The Opening of Walt Disney World Resort

Chapter 17: Walt Disney's Contribution to Art Education

Chapter 18: Walt Disney's Ultimate Legacy

Conclusion

Introduction

"All our dreams can come true, if we have the courage to pursue them."

Thank you for downloading this book, entitled "The Life of Walter Elias Disney." It will provide you with an in-depth look at the life and career of Walt Disney; a man who did the impossible time and time again. His positive outlook on life will hopefully inspire you to go out and do something that others think you cannot achieve.

Walt Disney is a name known across the world, despite the fact he died in 1966, long before many of his current fans were even born. He started off as a talented artist and transformed into a brilliant businessman who was able to translate the ideas in his head into reality. The legacy he has left for children and many adults is ongoing and shows no sign of dying out.

The Disney family is no longer involved with the running of the Walt Disney Company, but they are still following the dream that Walt himself started. Today, the company is headed by Robert A. Iger who has taken the company to new levels of success with its acquisitions of Pixar, Marvel and Lucasfilm. This brought the company to the forefront of the entertainment industry and cemented its already strong reputation. The leadership is reluctant to sit on its laurels, however, and still has plenty of plans to create the best content possible by using the latest technology out there.

Of course, the main things that people remember about Disney are his characters and films, particularly Mickey Mouse and Steamboat Willie and Snow White and the Seven Dwarves. But it is not just for on-screen entertainment that Disney is famous; it is still the dream of many young children to visit Disneyland in California and the Walt Disney World resort in Orlando. There, children can come face to face with their favorite Disney characters; some of them old ones like Mickey Mouse and Daffy Duck, others of them more current ones like Anna the Ice Princess and Buzz Lightyear.

This book will chronicle how Walt Disney grew up and how his talent as an artist was encouraged by his family and friends. It will illustrate how he became successful, despite much trial and error in the early days, yet managed to do the impossible again and again. It will show how he came to make such a mark on the American public, and, by extension, the rest of the world. Most importantly of all, it will show you, the reader, how success does not always happen overnight, that mistakes will be made along the way, but if you are brave and soldier on, hard work and some talent can result in success.

At the same time, it is important to never forget the past. As Walt Disney he said:

"I only hope that we don't lose sight of one thing – that it was all started by a mouse."

His humility, and focus on family, ensured that he never forgot where he came from and how hard he had to work in order to build up the Disney Empire. This book will look at his success in detail and will suggest ways that readers can use his experience to make a success of their own lives, whether their ambition is to build something of the size of the Walt Disney Company, or just to have a happy and secure lifestyle.

Chapter 1: Early Childhood Years

"All the adversity I've had in my life, all my troubles and obstacles, have strengthened me... You may not realize it when it happens, but a kick in the teeth may be the best thing in the world for you."

Walt Disney was born Walter Elias Disney in a tiny wooden house in Chicago, Illinois, on December 5, 1901. His parents were Elias Disney and Flora Call. He was named after a friend of his father, Walter Parr, who was the minister at the local St. Paul Congregational Church.

Elias Disney

Elias Disney was Canadian-Irish; his grandfather (Walt's great-grandfather) had immigrated to Canada from County Kilkenny in Ireland in 1801. Walt's great-grandfather's name was Arundel Elias Disney and his family was descended from a man who had accompanied William the Conqueror to England in 1066; his name was Robert D'Isigny. The name later became anglicized to Disney.

Elias Disney moved to America from Ontario, Canada in 1878, initially trying his luck with gold panning in California, before moving to Kansas, where his parents had already settled. He met and married Flora Call, of English and German descent, in 1888. By the time the twentieth century began, Elias was a building contractor who built a number of properties in Chicago, including the St. Paul Congregational Church. He was a very religious man; he was a trustee of the church and his wife, Flora, was the treasurer.

The house in which Walt Disney was born and which was built by his father in 1893 still exists. There are plans to make it into a museum of his childhood. It was bought by a couple in 2013 and they plan to renovate it with funds collected through crowdfunding. The house, when completed, will not be an official Disney attraction, but Walt Disney's great-nephew, Roy Disney, has given his blessings to the plan. It is not yet clear when the museum will be completed, but when it is, it is expected to look just as it did when Walt Disney himself lived there, providing visitors with the opportunity to see his humble beginnings first-hand.

Flora Call Disney

Flora Call, Walt's mother was born in Steuben, Ohio, and was a neighbor of Elias Disney's father. She was very different in temperament from her husband, who was very religious and short-tempered. Flora was lively and loved playing with her children, which is believed to have encouraged Walt Disney and his talent for drawing. Ironically, she died at the age of 70 having moved to a home in California bought for her by Walt and Roy Disney. A faulty furnace caused her to die of asphyxiation in 1938. Elias Disney died just two years later.

Walt was one of five children; he had three brothers, Herbert, Raymond and Roy, all older than him, and one sister, Ruth, who was the youngest child. He was particularly close to his brother, Roy, who encouraged him as he grew up and with whom Walt eventually went into business when he moved to Kansas in his twenties. All the Disney brothers and sister were to have long lives; Walt was the youngest to die at just 66, while Raymond died at 98 and Ruth died at 91.

The Marceline years

The Disney family didn't stay for long in Chicago. Some people believe that Elias was worried about the high rate of crime there and wanted a safer place in which to bring up his children. When Walt was just four years of age, the Disney family moved to a farm in Marceline, Missouri. Elias' brother, Robert, had bought some farmland there and Elias and his family joined him there to earn a living.

Walt Disney spent the formative part of his childhood in Marceline and was very happy there. It was in Marceline that he learned to draw and was given plenty of opportunity to put his talent into practice. A family friend, a retired doctor offered Walt money to draw his horse and Walt used to copy the front page cartoons of the newspaper to which Elias Disney subscribed. He also spent a lot of time in lessons doodling, rather than listening to his teacher, and he once painted picture on the side of the family house with tar.

Walt Disney started an interest in trains while he was in Marceline, something that remained with his for the rest of his life. His uncle, Mike Martin, worked as a train engineer for the Sante Fe railroad that ran close to the family farm. Walt and his brother would wait until they heard the sound of the train and would run to a clearing from which they could see and wave to the train. Uncle Mike would often be able to see them and would wave back.

Walt's interest in the railway was cemented when he worked one summer for the railroad selling refreshments to the customers. He loved the freedom that he felt while on board and spent many happy times in his adulthood trying to recreate that feeling by designing and building model railways. It was also during his time in Marceline that Walt saw his first movie. It was about the crucifixion and left a real impression on him. However, it was drawing that really colored his time in Marceline.

Although he much preferred drawing to lessons, Walt did go to school, but not until 1909, when he and his sister Ruth attended Marceline's Park School. Before that, he had no formal schooling, although it is likely that the strict attitude of his father ensured that he did some lessons at home. It is believed that it was primarily the encouragement of his mother, Flora, and brother, Roy, which kept him interested in drawing. Disney's older brothers, Herbert and Ray, had already run away from Marceline in 1908, looking for ways to make money. They found their way back to Chicago, where they found work as clerks.

Back to Kansas

Sadly, the family's time in Marceline was limited because the farm failed and Elias became ill with typhoid fever and then pneumonia. By the end of 1910, he had sold the farm and was looking for another way to make a living. Initially, the family rented a home in Marceline before moving to Kansas in 1911. However, Walt would never forget his time in Marceline and the feeling of freedom that being amongst nature gave him.

Chapter 2: Walt Disney's Teenage Years

"It's kind of fun to do the impossible."

By 1911, Walt had moved back to Kansas with his family. Although Marceline left a great impression on him, he also enjoyed being in Kansas. The family initially rented a property on East Thirty-First Street, but eventually moved to a property on Bellefontaine Street.

Elias Disney bought a Kansas City Star newspaper delivery route and gave Roy and Walt the task of delivering newspapers. They delivered to about 700 customers. Elias also arranged the delivery of eggs and milk to his customers, which were imported from a farm in Marceline. It is perhaps from his father that Walt learned that, when things didn't quite work out, it was just a matter of rethinking goals and trying something else.

Walt found the work exhausting and often struggled to stay awake at class. He got up at 4.30 in the morning and worked until it was time to go to school; he then had to go straight back on the delivery route when school was over. His grades, as a result, were poor. At the time, he was attending the Benton Grammar School, along with his sister Ruth. He had already completed the second grade while still in Marceline, but was forced to repeat the grade. He also studied art classes at the Kansas City Art Institute on Saturdays.

While at Benton Grammar School, he became close friends with Walter Pfeiffer, whose family loved the theater. They introduced Walt to vaudeville and motion pictures. As a result, as well as practicing his art, Walt developed a talent for performing and often entertained his classmates and friends by imitating Charlie Chaplin.

He also developed a great knack for storytelling and was often invited by his teacher to tell his classmates a story, while illustrating it on the blackboard. As he grew older, he would steal out of the house at night, without his father's knowledge, to perform skits in local theaters. This all helped to develop his interest in the entertainment industry as a whole and helped shape his future career.

By 1917, Elias Disney had sold his newspaper delivery route and took a more active role in the management of the O-Zell Company of Chicago, a company in which he had been invested for years. The family moved to rented accommodation in Ogden Avenue. By this time, Walt Disney had moved to McKinley High School. He was able to take classes in photography and drawing, and drew cartoons for the school newspaper. However, he didn't really enjoy school and wanted to leave as soon as possible.

At the same time, Walt took evening classes at the Chicago Academy of Fine Arts, where he took classes led by Louis Grell. Grell was a portrait artist and professor at the Chicago Academy of Fine Arts from 1916 to 1922. He must have been impressed by Walt Disney's artistic talent because he often spoke of him to his family, but refused to speak to anyone outside of the family. Grell later became a professor at the Art Institute of Chicago.

The War years

By the time Walt was 16, World War I had broken out. At the time, Walt was still at McKinley High School, but had already decided that he wanted to drop out. According to the Walt Disney Family Museum friend, Russell Maas, and they had put a down-payment on a movie camera. However, stories about the war, particularly from Walt's older brothers Ray and Roy, made them decide that they also wanted to play their part.

Unfortunately, at just 16 years of age, Walt and Russell were a year below the minimum age limit and the Navy turned them down. They then decided to try for the Canadian armed forces, but Russell's poor eyesight precluded him and Walt decided that he didn't want to go on his own. Then they heard about the Red Cross Ambulance Corps and decided to apply for work with them, providing false names in their application. Unfortunately, they were told that they needed signatures from their parents in order to get passports.

Russell's mother found his suitcase and realized that the boys were planning to run away. She shared her fears with Flora Disney, who confronted Walt. He confessed and explained the situation. Elias Disney was furious and refused to sign the papers, but Flora softened. Three of her sons had already left home in the middle of the night and she was concerned about losing her last son without her permission too. She therefore signed the papers on Elias' behalf, much to his anger. Walt changed his birth year to 1900 and eventually enlisted in the Ambulance Corps, along with Russell, in 1918.

It appears that Walt wasn't aware of the horrors that war could bring because his letters only shared his excitement at being part of the war effort. It is perhaps lucky that he became very ill, having contracted influenza while training, and had to move back home to recuperate. His mother, also ill, still managed to nurse him through the illness. When Walt had recovered his senses, he learned that Russell Maas had already been sent off to France, along with some of his other friends.

Walt was assigned to another training base, but Walt thought his plans were thwarted yet again when the Armistice was signed on November 11, 1918. However, there was still a need for ambulance drivers overseas and, as a result, Walt was sent off to France, arriving the day before his 17th birthday. However, he had little opportunity to meet the sick and injured, finding himself assigned the role of tour guide to visiting officials, something he was very good at.

Walt also used his talent at drawing by sending letters to his old school friends and by drawing caricatures for his friends to send home, thereby earning some extra money. However, he was also beginning to get homesick and by August 1919, he had put in for a discharge. He met up with Russell Haas again in Paris, where they made plans to sail down the Mississippi on a raft. Unfortunately, they were unable to travel home together and a dock strike in Marseille kept Walt behind for another 23 days.

Eventually, Walt returned home to Chicago on October 10, 1919. Ready for yet more adventure on the Mississippi, Walt was disappointed to find that Russell had met a girl and was no longer willing to be his accomplice. It was time for Walt Disney to start making his own plans – even though what he was about to do shocked his father and was far from being conventional.

Chapter 3: The Kansas Years – 1920 – 1923

"I only hope that we don't lose sight of one thing – that it was all started by a mouse."

By 1919, Walt Disney was back in Chicago and was ready to start the next stage in his life. His father wanted him to work for the O-Zell company, in the hope that he could make a career out of it. Walt, however, wanted to make his own way and refused to let his father interfere. He was no longer a boy; he had grown up while in France, and knew exactly what he wanted to do – forge a career as a cartoonist. Perhaps in order to escape his father's influence, he moved to Kansas City.

Unfortunately, things didn't go quite according to plan. Although Walt looked for work, both as a cartoonist and as an ambulance driver, he couldn't find work as either. Struggling to survive, he turned to his brother, Roy, for help. At the time, Roy was working in a local bank and managed to get Walt work at the Pesman-Rubin Art Studio. There, Walt honed his artistic skills by creating advertisements for movie theaters, newspapers and magazines. Perhaps most importantly, he met and became friends with Ubbe Iwerks, another cartoonist.

Ubbe Iwerks

Ub Iwerks was extremely talented, but, unlike Walt Disney, was a very reserved man. He needed the outgoing nature and business acumen of Disney in order to succeed. Together, they started a company in 1920 called Iwerks-Disney Commercial Artists. Unfortunately, the company wasn't to last very long. Disney soon found that he wasn't earning enough money and was forced to take work with the Kansas City Film Ad Company. Iwerks initially stayed with Iwerks-Disney, but found that he couldn't run the business on his own. In the meantime, Walt convinced Kansas City Film Ad Company to give Iwerks a job and he eventually joined Walt working there.

At this stage, both friends were showing great interest in animation, which was still in its beginning stages. They both studied the technique and made plans to use it at some point in the near future.

Although Walt and Ub were very different people, they were close friends. In a biography of Walt Disney by Barbara Ford, she explained that Walt used to tease Ub mercilessly, doing things like locking him in the bathroom and sending him postcards signed by girls. Ub was extremely nervous around women and was probably very embarrassed by all this, but he never complained and the two were so close that, instead of drawing up contracts, they agreed on deals by just shaking hands.

Laugh-O-Gram Films

Just like his father, Walt Disney needed constant challenge and soon became bored working for the Kansas City Film Ad Company. He therefore decided to form a new company in 1922 – called Laugh-O-Gram Films. This was a film studio located on East Thirty-First Street in Kansas City. Iwerks initially went with him – they used the remaining money from Iwerks-Disney Commercial Artists to fund Laugh-O-Grams. Walt came up with a character called Professor Whosis who told jokes in between movies. The character became so popular that Walt was asked to provide more and more material. He went on to make his first film, an animated version of Red Riding Hood, a story that his mother had read to him as a child. That was followed by Puss in Boots. Investors showed interest, but the money wasn't really forthcoming and Iwerks eventually went back to the Kansas City Film Ad Company.

By this time, the company was in dire straits and Walt was forced to live in the office to make ends meet. He took baths once a week at Union Station. He thought his problems were over when a Kansas dentist offered him $500 for a short film showing the benefits of cleaning teeth.

Walt then started making Alice's Comedies, a series of shorts in which a little girl called Alice and a cat called Julius had adventures in a fantasy world. The shorts were only ten minutes long and Walt hoped it would resolve the film studio's financial problems, but unfortunately, that was never to happen. The studio was soon in such financial difficulties that it went bankrupt – sadly, the high quality of the film was accompanied by high wages for its employees and the studio simply didn't earn enough to pay them. By July 1923, the studio was no longer in existence and Walt was forced to put his plans for success on hold – although not for long.

Mickey Mouse

Walt's experience at Laugh-O-Gram Studios didn't go to waste. He learned, from hard experience, that ideas of success don't necessarily translate into reality and that, if he was to make a success of his career, he would have to learn to be more careful with money. He also came up with the initial plans for Mickey Mouse, inspired by a little mouse that used to appear in the studio. The mouse became so tame that Walt trained it to run around on his drawing board. When he had to leave the studios, he was so sad to have to leave the mouse behind that

he took it to a safe neighborhood and set it free.

In 1928, when married to his wife, Lillian, he showed her a sketch of the mouse and said that he was planning to call it Mortimer Mouse. She said Mortimer was "too sissified" and suggested that he call it Mickey Mouse instead. And so Mickey Mouse was born from a tiny brown mouse Walt Disney befriended while at Laugh-O-Gram Studios.

However, for all the experience he had gained at Laugh-O-Gram Studios, Walt decided that it was time to leave Kansas and try his luck in Hollywood. He sold his movie camera, which gave him enough money to buy a one-way ticket, and made his way to Hollywood to set up a company with his brother, Roy, who was already in Hollywood.

Ub Iwerks didn't go with him, but waved him off at the station. However, this wasn't to be the end of the Iwerks-Disney collaboration because Iwerks was eventually to join him in Hollywood. Iwerks would never become as famous as Disney, but seemed quite happy to remain in the shadows as one of Walt's closest friends.

It was by making friends with people like Iwerks that Walt managed to pull off so many coups in his later life. He recognized talent when he saw it, but was also prepared to put in the time and energy to make friends and then use his influence to encourage them to go on and do great things alongside him.

Chapter 4: The Hollywood Years – 1923 – 1928

"If you can dream it, you can do it."

When Walt moved to Hollywood, he decided to start a company with his brother and close friend, Roy. Together, they set up the Disney Brothers Studio in their Uncle Robert's garage with just $750. However, they knew that they needed to move out of the garage as soon as possible. Fortunately, Walt had a great idea.

The Alice Comedies

When Walt left Kansas, he took with him the reel of The Alice Comedies, for which he hoped would be able to find a distributor. He did. He wrote to Margaret Winkler, a New York distributor, who wanted to do a distribution deal for more films based on the Alice in Wonderland stories. Finally, Walt was in business. He asked Virginia Davis, who had provided the voice for Alice, and Ub Iwerks and his family to relocate to Hollywood which they did. The studio moved from Uncle Robert's garage to an office at the back of a real estate office and started making more Alice films. In 1925, the studio was moved again, to an address in the Silver Lake district of Los Angeles.

The Alice shorts are now in the public domain, but are quite shocking when compared with today's cartoons. Although Alice is a little girl, she faces peril on a regular basis, including being tied to a log about to be cut in half by a sawmill, and kidnapped by cruel villains. However, for the time, this appeared to be completely acceptable, and the shorts were very popular. However, by 1927, the shorts had outrun their time and were drawn to a close. That didn't matter though, because Walt Disney had plenty of other plans up his sleeve. Unfortunately they weren't all to lead to the success that he first hoped.

Oswald the Lucky Rabbit

Charles Mintz, who worked alongside Margaret Winkler, ordered a new animated series to be distributed through Universal Pictures. The series was to star Oswald the Lucky Rabbit. Oswald was a rabbit with a quirky sense of humor, drawn and created by the brilliant Ub Iwerks. Universal chose the name of Oswald, while the character of a rabbit was chosen because there were too many other cat-themed cartoons around at the time, such as Felix the Cat.

The first cartoon, Poor Papa, was rejected because Universal thought that Oswald was too old and that the production quality wasn't good enough. Walt and Ub Iwerks returned to the drawing board and came up with Trolley Troubles, which was eventually released in September 1927. The all-animated series was an instant success. Poor Papa was eventually released in 1928 after having been updated.

Unfortunately, trouble was on the horizon. Walt Disney traveled to New York to meet with Charles Mintz in the spring of 1928 to negotiate a better deal. He was shocked to find that not only was Mintz not willing to negotiate, he suggested that Disney Brothers should take a cut and told him that it was Universal Pictures and not Disney Brothers who owned the Oswald trademark. Walt refused and, as a result, lost his animation staff with the exception of Ub Iwerks. Universal and Mintz went on to make more Oswald shorts. However, Disney had plenty of other ideas.

Mickey Mouse Returns

While on the train journey back to Los Angeles, Walt Disney

remembered his time in Kansas and the little mouse that had kept him company. When back in the studio, he shared his ideas with Ub Iwerks and the two Disney brothers, Iwerks and their wives collaborated to come up with a new cartoon character – Mickey Mouse. Iwerks came up with new ideas for the character, primarily to make him easier to animate, but it was Walt himself who gave Mickey his voice and continued to do so until 1947.

Disney Brothers made two silent shorts featuring Mickey Mouse; Plane Crazy and Gallopin' Goucho. However, the company failed to find distributors, probably because the shorts were silent. Walt Disney refused to admit defeat and opted to make a cartoon with sound entitled Steamboat Willie.

Steamboat Willie features Mickey Mouse as the captain of a steamboat. Mickey, however, is not the real captain and when the real captain, Pete, arrives on scene, he is not pleased to find Mickey in his role. Chaos ensues. Mickey is eventually joined by Minnie Mouse, who brings a guitar and some sheet music, which are eaten by the goat. However, they still manage to make some music, until Pete gives Mickey some chores to do. Mickey is unrepentant and soon finds something else to amuse him.

Disney Brothers managed to find themselves a distributor in the form of Pat Powers, a businessman, who also managed to get them access to a sound-synchronization process called Cinephone. Pat Powers had stolen the idea for this from another company, but that was not a problem for Disney Brothers, although Powers later had to face the music.

Steamboat Willie premièred in New York in 1928 and was an instant success. It initially had a run of two weeks and earned Disney Brothers $500 a week, which at the time was a lot of money. It was a hit with the public for many reasons – it had sound, great music, the production was of a high quality and, most of all, the public found it funny. Plane Crazy and Gallopin' Gaucho were later released as cartoons with a soundtrack and were also hugely popular.

Walt Disney hadn't just made a name for himself in the United States; his skills had also been noticed in other countries. Variety magazine said that although Steamboat Willie wasn't the first cartoon to feature sound, it was the best cartoon so far that had featured sound and that there was no doubt the product quality was first-class. Walt Disney and Disney Brothers were well on the way to the success that they had always dreamed of.

Chapter 5: Walt Disney – The Family Man

"A man should never neglect his family for business."

Although Walt Disney had been busy forging his career in the 1920s, he still found some time for his private life. In 1925, Walt Disney met, and married, his wife, Lillian Bounds. They were to remain married until his death in 1966.

Lillian Disney

Lillian Marie Bounds was born in 1899 in Spalding, Idaho. She grew up on an Indian reservation where her father was a blacksmith and federal marshal. She showed a great interest in art and, in 1925, was hired to work at the Disney Brothers studio. Slim and pretty, with brown hair, she soon caught Walt's attention and, when giving the girls from the studio a lift home, would always make sure that he dropped Lillian off last. Walt was not like many men in Hollywood; he wasn't interested in Hollywood starlets and he liked the fact that Lillian understood the meaning of hard work. According to the website, Hollywoodstories.com, she loved the fact that he was so kind and gentle around women, even if he did swear a lot when he was around his animators.

After a brief courtship, the couple married in 1925. Walt's parents were unable to attend the wedding ceremony, and Lillian's father was already dead, so her uncle gave her away. Lillian was wearing a dress that she had made for herself because she earned just fifteen dollars a week; a far cry from the financial situation she would find herself in in later life.

Lillian wasn't a wife who would sit quietly at home waiting for her husband's return. She continued to work as an artist and was credited for her work on Plane Crazy. She spent a lot of time listening to him and his ideas and, once she knew him well enough, was quick to criticize if she didn't agree with him. It was her idea to name Mickey Mouse Mickey and not Mortimer. However, there were other ideas that she disagreed with that Walt went ahead with anyway – and then reminded Lillian that she had been wrong. For example, she didn't think that Snow White and the Seven Dwarfs would be the huge hit that it was.

Nevertheless, Lillian loved Walt and the life that he made for her. Even when the studios were having financial problems, he made life as easy as possible for Lillian. With him, she enjoyed many holidays abroad and even put up with his drinking habit, which he developed to numb the pain of a riding accident. She was sometimes jealous of the time that he spent working, but she never doubted that he was faithful to her.

Walt and Lillian were still married when Walt succumbed to illness and died in 1966. She, however, went on to live to the grand old age of 98 and even remarried to John L. Truyens, whom she also outlived. With Walt, she had two daughters, one of whom was adopted, and several grandchildren.

Lillian died in 1997, exactly 31 years to the day after Walt Disney died. She is buried next to him.

Diane Disney Miller
Lillian Disney's first two pregnancies tragically ended in miscarriages, so when Lillian was finally able to carry a pregnancy to term, the

couple was delighted. Diane Disney Miller was born Diane Marie Disney on December 1933. When she was born, Walt Disney was already so famous that the Los Angeles Times announced that "Mickey Mouse has a daughter." She largely kept out of the limelight until her death in 2013 at the age of 79.

According to an obituary in The Guardian, Diane is remembered primarily for two things; it is because of her introduction to P.L. Travers' book, Mary Poppins, that Walt was encouraged to pursue the film rights and, in accompanying his daughters to a theme park, Walt was first inspired to come up with the ideas for Disneyland. He wanted to create a theme park that was fun for all the family and not just children.

One of the few times that Diane Disney Miller came out of hiding was in 1993, when she and her mother both spoke out in public to champion Walt Disney. A biography entitled Walt Disney: Hollywood's Dark Prince was published by Marc Eliot. Both Diane and Lillian disputed the basis on which the book was written – that Walt Disney was an FBI informer who had difficult relationships with a number of people.

Diane married Ron Miller, a professional athlete, and had seven children with him - Christopher, Joanna, Tamara, Jennifer, Walter, Ronald and Patrick. They would go on to provide her with thirteen grandchildren.

Sharon Mae Lund

In 1937, Lillian miscarried once more and the couple decided to adopt a two-week-old baby girl whom they named Sharon Mae Disney. She was born on December 21, 1936 and soon became a much-loved part of the family. Lillian didn't even want it known that she was adopted, because she wanted Sharon to think that she was born to the family, but somehow the press found out.

Like Diane, Sharon kept herself very private and rarely spoke out about her father, although both she and Diane have mentioned the importance that Walt Disney placed on family and that he was always around for school functions, even when they tried to persuade him that he didn't need to go.

Sharon married Robert Borgfeldt Brown when she was 22 and together, they had a baby daughter, Victoria. Sadly Brown died in 1967 from lung cancer. Reluctant to marry again, Sharon spent a few years in mourning before she remarried – this time to William S. Lund. She went on to have two more children with him – twins Michelle and Brad Lund. Sharon herself died from cancer in 1993 and her daughter, Victoria, died at a young age from health complications. Neither Michelle nor Brad have children and have been embroiled in a lawsuit against each other over their inheritance. It is perhaps a good thing that Walt Disney didn't live to see this happen.

Sharon left a donation of $11 million to the California Institute of the Arts, which went on to create the Sharon D. Lund School of Dance.

Chapter 6: Silly Symphonies and Early Success in the 1930s

"Disneyland is a work of love. We didn't go into Disneyland just with the idea of making money."

Back in 1929, Walt Disney's career was going very well. Mickey Mouse had been very well received as a character and made Walt Disney and Disney Brothers famous across the world. However, Walt Disney was never one to rest on his laurels and by 1929, he was looking for another project. He came up with Silly Symphonies, a series of short cartoons set to music, which would prove to be another success for the Disney camp, even though they did not introduce recurring characters.

The Skeleton Dance

A series of shorts, the first of which was The Skeleton Dance, was released in 1929. The Skeleton Dance revolves around four skeletons in a graveyard who decide to make some music using their own skeletons and dance around. After a night of merriment, they suddenly realize that it is time for sunrise and make a dash to get back to their graves. The music was written by Carl Stalling, although he adapted part of Edvard Grieg's "The March of the Trolls" for part of the dance.

The Skeleton Dance was drawn and animated exclusively by Ub Iwerks, who was responsible for most of the Disney output at the time. However, Walt Disney didn't think Pat Powers, the distributor, was getting them enough money and, after negotiation with Columbia Pictures, Columbia became the new distributor.

Despite Disney's success, Walt was very aware of the competition and the need to keep ahead in the quality stakes. Despite the fact that the Silly Symphonies and Mickey Mouse were popular, there were other competitors who were edging in, including Max Fleischer, who was responsible for animating Betty Boop.

By 1932, Walt Disney had fallen out with the management of Columbia Pictures and turned to United Artists, who took over the distribution of Silly Symphonies. However, as a kickback, United Artists insisted that Disney somehow allowed Mickey Mouse to be associated with them. This he did by title cards and posters that featured Mickey Mouse.

Flowers and Trees

The move to United Artists proved to be a good one and the Silly Symphonies became even more popular. At the time, Dr. Herbert Kalmus had come up with the three-strip, full-color Technicolor process which replaced the previous two-tone Technicolor process and allowed the Silly Symphonies to be displayed even more fantastically. Walt then signed a contract with Technicolor, which gave Disney full rights to the process until the end of 1935.

During this time, Flowers and Trees, the latest Silly Symphony, which was already almost complete, had to be totally redone in full-color. The results were spectacular and the Symphony was an immediate hit. Disney won an Academy Award for Flowers and Trees in 1932. In the short, it is springtime and the flowers, trees and mushrooms are coming alive. Two trees, one of which is hollow and not very healthy-looking while the other is young and virile, vie for the attentions of a female tree. In the process, they manage to start a fire.

The Three Little Pigs

Other Silly Symphonies also did very well; in fact, The Three Little Pigs, based on the popular fairy tale and released in 1933, became the most successful cartoon short of all time. The Three Little Pigs also featured a song that would become hugely popular during the Great Depression and still remains popular today – "Who's Afraid of the Big Bad Wolf?" Disney Brothers were no longer just concentrating on technique; they were also ensuring that the stories behind the cartoons, no matter how short, had substance.

The Three Little Pigs story revolves around three little pigs called Practical Pig, Fiddler Pig and Fifer Pig. They all play instruments – Practical Pig plays the piano and Fiddler Pig and Fifer Pig obviously play the fiddle and the fife. All three pigs are building their own homes; however, Practical Pig takes the time to build his carefully with brick, whereas the other two use straw and sticks. As is to be expected, the Wolf comes along and quickly destroys the houses made of straw and sticks. Yet he can't do anything with the house of bricks and eventually ends up in a pot of boiling water in Practical Pig's fireplace.

Other Silly Symphonies

As the Encyclopedia of Animated Disney Shorts website explains, there were 75 Silly Symphonies made between 1929 and 1939. Some of the most successful Silly Symphonies included The Grasshopper and the Ants, The Tortoise and the Hare, Wynken Blyken and Nod, The Ugly Duckling and The Old Mill. The Old Mill was the first short to use the multi-plane camera technique, illustrating that, even during a short space of time, Disney Brothers were making use of all the technology they could get their hands on.

Three shorts were farmed out to animators Rudy Ising and Hugh Harman, who were both involved with Walt Disney when he set up Laugh-O-Gram in Kansas City. In the late 1930s, they were both working as freelancers and were happy to do contract work for Disney Brothers whenever they were needed. They put together three shorts, entitled Merbabies, Pipe Dreams and The Little Bantamweight.

Of the three shorts, Disney only bought Merbabies, which is set underwater and involves some very happy baby mermaids who take part in some circus antics on the ocean floor. They are eventually blown to the surface and disappear into the waves. This is the first piece of Disney animation that wasn't actually made by Disney.

The other two shorts, Pipe Dreams and The Little Bantamweight, were sold to MGM, which later released them as Happy Harmonies shorts. Ising and Harman were re-employed by MGM in 1939.

By 1939, Walt Disney thought that the success of Silly Symphonies had come to an end because of the popularity of feature-length films and so the company stopped making them. They were also facing competition from other series, such as MGM's Happy Harmonies and The Warner Bros' Looney Tunes and Merrie Melodies. There was no need to worry, however, because there was still plenty of work coming the Disney Brothers' way and in the coming years, the world of Disney would expand in ways that no one at the time could even begin to imagine.

Chapter 7: More Early Success – 1929 – 1939

"Disneyland will never be completed. It will continue to grow as long as there is imagination left in the world."

Although Silly Symphonies took up a large part of the Disney business in the 1930s, it was far from being the only success it had. Part of Walt Disney's charm was that he could recognize an opportunity when he saw it and, rather than sit back and enjoy himself, he encouraged the company to forge ahead with his plans. The result was some of his most famous work.

Mickey Mouse in Black and White

Following Mickey Mouse's debut in Steamboat Willie in 1929, Mickey Mouse was to feature in 130 films, most of which were shorts. Between 1929 and 1935, Mickey Mouse appeared in black and white, but would eventually make it into the world of color. The films came thick and fast.

In 1929, popular Mickey Mouse films included The Barn Dance, The Opry House, While the Cat's Away, The Barnyard Dance and The Karnival Kid. Mickey wore white gloves for the first time in The Opry House and would continue to do so for the rest of his 'career.' That was to distinguish his hands from the black of his body. The Karnival Kid is well-known for introducing Mickey's voice for the first time. Previously, nothing but grunts, whistles and laughs had been heard from him. His first words were "Hot dogs! Hot dogs!"

Sadly, in 1930, Walt Disney was to lose his top animator and best friend, Ub Iwerks, who was headhunted by Pat Powers when Powers and Disney fell out over finances. The last film to be made by Ub

Iwerks was The Cactus Kid. After that, Iwerks left to set up his own studio, something he had long wanted to do. However, although Iwerks was the creator of the original animated Mickey, Disney retained the rights and continued to work without Iwerks by finding new animators. Post-Iwerks, the Mickey Mouse films were created to Walt Disney himself, rather than both Iwerks and Disney. It was the end of an important collaboration for Walt, but fortunately, he had plenty of others, including his brother, Roy, on whom he could rely.

In 1932, Walt Disney received an Academy Award for the creation of Mickey Mouse, as well as a nomination for Mickey's Orphans, released in 1931. He was also beginning to make a name for other characters other than Mickey; Pluto first appeared in The Picnic and then again as Mickey's pet in The Moose Hunt. In fact, the Disney creators were finding it harder and harder to find original stories for Mickey himself. By 1934, Donald Duck, who had first appeared in a Silly Symphonies short, was introduced in Orphan's Benefit, was introduced into the Mickey Mouse series and soon became hugely popular.

Mickey Mouse in Color

By 1935, it was time for Mickey Mouse to appear in color and he did so to great effect in The Band Concert, in which Mickey is conducting the William Tell Overture when the entire orchestra is swept up by a tornado. To celebrate his color makeover, Walt Disney also partially redesigned Mickey. In 1994, this film was voted the third best piece of animation ever by animation professionals, so it is no wonder that, in 1935, it was such a hit with Disney fans. Disney was also given an award by the League of Nations in 1935 for creating Mickey. Iincluded Mickey's Fire Brigade, Moose Hunters, Clock Cleaners,

Although Mickey was still hugely popular, by 1938, Donald Duck was starting to surpass his popularity. Some of the most successful films of the period featured Mickey Mouse, Donald Duck and Goofy and Lonesome Ghosts, Boat Builders and Mickey's Trailer.

In 1939, Mickey was to receive yet another redesign. Fred Moore gave him white eyes with pupils (rather than all-black eyes), pink–colored skin and a plumper shaped body. These changes were displayed in 1939's The Pointer, perhaps getting him ready for his first feature film, which would be Fantasia in 1940.

Snow White and the Seven Dwarfs

Another huge piece of Disney success of the 1930s was the Disney version of Snow White and the Seven Dwarfs. By 1934, Walt had successfully created two animated series; Silly Symphonies and Mickey Mouse. He was now ready to do something a little meatier. He wanted to make a feature-length animation out of Snow White and the Seven Dwarfs and started to plan the project. Both his brother, Roy, and wife, Lillian, tried to talk him out of it, but he didn't want to listen.

To prepare his staff for the animation, Disney called in an art professor to train his staff. As a result, the staff started work in 1935, but were slowed down in 1937 when Disney ran out of funding. Fortunately, by showing a rough cut of the film to managers at the Bank of America, Disney was able to secure enough funding for the film to be completed.

The premiere of Snow White and the Seven Dwarfs was shown at the Carthay Circle Theater on December 21, 1937. It was an immediate success, with the audience rising to their feet to applaud Disney's efforts. It was released in Technicolor in 1938 to continuing success. Disney won a total of eight Oscars for Snow White and the Seven Dwarfs and the film made over $8 million on its initial release.

Unhappily, the huge success of Snow White and the Seven Dwarfs was undermined by the death of Walt's mother, Flora. Roy and Walt moved their parents to a new home close to the studios so that they could enjoy first-hand the fruits of their sons' success. Soon after moving in, Flora died of asphyxiation, attributed to a faulty furnace.

Walt was to learn that along with success, tragedy sometimes occurs and, although he didn't let his mother's death thwart him in his desire to remain at the top of the entertainment industry, he did feel guilty for years. His father was unaffected by the fumes given out by the furnace, but would die anyway within a couple of years.

Walt reacted by throwing himself into his work and soon had a number of other projects in the works, some of which would prove to be more successful than others. One of Walt's strengths was his ability to turn disaster or disappointment into something productive. He proved himself able to do this time and time again.

Chapter 8: Disney Brothers' Success and Failure – 1939 – 1941

"The flower that blooms in adversity is the rarest and most beautiful of all."

In the first stages of World War II, Disney Brothers was at an all-time high following the success of Snow White and the Seven Dwarfs. It really seemed as if Walt Disney could do no wrong. The money earned from the film enabled the Disney studios to build a new studio in Burbank and, in 1939, the company was able to move into new offices.

However, with the world in uproar, it was perhaps obvious that the fallout of World War II would eventually affect the success of Disney. Although America didn't become involved in the war until 1941, Europe was an important market for Disney films and products and, as embroiled as it was in war, the European market became virtually non-existent. Nevertheless, Walt wasn't willing to sit by and wait until the war was over, so he fought on.

Burbank Studios

Walt Disney realized that the continuing success of Disney studios meant that they needed to move into a building that was representative of his achievements. With the profits made from Snow White and the Seven Dwarfs, he therefore decided to put down a deposit on 51 acres of land on Burbank, where he intended to have a modern day animation studio built.

Rather than leaving the process to the architect and interior designers, Walt was involved with every stage of the proceedings and wanted to have the final say on everything inside and outside the building. He wanted the studios to be state-of-the-art and to provide everything that was necessary to make animated films.

According to Studioservices.go.com, at the center of the lot was the Animation Building, which would be the home of the painters and animators. There was also to be inking and Painting building and the Camera building, which is where the finishing touches to the animation was done and then photographed. Then there was the Cutting building, which is where the post-production process took place. This included dubbing, scoring, voice recording and special effects.

Walt was keen that the making of Disney films was not stopped by anything, including the weather. He therefore asked for a series of underground tunnels to be made so that the employees could go about their business without getting wet. All the utilities attached to the studios were also underground. The result was a campus for Disney staff.

The employees moved into their new premises on December 24, 1939. They were not, however, given much time to enjoy their new space because there were several projects in the pipeline that they needed to work on – most pressingly, Pinocchio and Fantasia, both of which were due to be released in 1940.

Pinocchio

After the success of Snow White and the Seven Dwarfs, there were great expectations for Pinocchio and Fantasia. Neither of them quite lived up to these expectations.

Pinocchio was the second feature film that Disney made. Although it is hard to believe now, the film made a loss when it was first released; it is only afterwards that the film became a success. Based on the story of a little wooden puppet who wanted to become a little boy, it is told by Jiminy Cricket. The film is accompanied by a series of songs, including "When I Wish upon a Star," which won an Academy Award in 1940 for Best Original Song.

The effects animation in the film was second to none. Effects animators are responsible for making everything in an animation move, not just the characters. As a result, the film included thunder, lightning, smoke and science fiction effects.

When the film was released, it was generally considered to be a success. However, the film made a loss of $94,000, which, for the time, was a great deal of money. There are a number of reasons for this, including the high production costs due to the technology used to make them look so spectacular, the use of high profile actors to voice the main characters and the fact that World War II had cut off the European market.

Walt Disney was deeply depressed by this, but the worst was yet to come.

Fantasia

Fantasia, featuring Mickey Mouse, was meant as a comeback for the character, who had lost some of his popularity in the late 1930s. It was based around a short that had initially been made for the Silly Symphonies series – The Sorcerer's Apprentice. However, production costs were higher than Walt knew it could earn. He therefore had the idea of making it part of a feature-length film consisting of eight sections in all. In each of the eight sections, a piece of classical music is played, against which the characters perform, which included:

Toccata and Fugue in D Minor by Johann Sebastian Bach

Nutcracker Suite by Pyotr Ilyich Tchaikovsky

The Sorcerer's Apprentice by Paul Dukas

Rite of spring by Igor Stravinsky

Intermission – during which the orchestra had a jam session

The Pastoral Symphony by Ludwig van Beethoven

Dance of the Hours by Amilcare Ponchielli

Night on Bald Mountain by Modest Mussorgsky and Ave Maria by Franz Schubert

Disney sound engineers, working with RCA, led to the development of Fantasound, which involved two projectors playing at the same time. The result was amazing – but then it should have been because a fifth of the film's budget was spent on the sound recording.

The public reaction to Fantasia was great, but even though the box office brought in high profits, they didn't make up for the production costs and Disney was forced to extend existing loans. Even worse, Europe was in the middle of a World War and so Fantasia didn't make it to Europe, which would have made up nearly half of the profits from the film. As a result, Fantasia made an even greater loss than Pinocchio, adding to Disney's frustration. Fortunately, there was good news ahead.

Dumbo

Dumbo was primarily made to help win back some of the losses that had been made with Fantasia. Disney's aim was to keep the production as simple as possible. The story was based on the story by Helen Aberson. It revolves around a circus elephant, Jumbo Jr, whose large ears lead to him being teased and nicknamed Dumbo. His only real friend is a mouse called Timothy. Of course, Dumbo wins through, in the way that only the characters of Disney movies can.

Dumbo was originally only supposed to be a short film, but as Walt started to plan for it, he realized that the only way to do it justice was to make it into a feature-length film. He also saw it as a possible savior, following the loss made by Fantasia. The supervising director was told to keep the film as simple as possible and he did so. The animators were therefore less caught up in detail and more able to concentrate on making the story a really good one.

However, the production of Dumbo was not without its challenges. Disney studio staff went on strike because of a union issue and, for five weeks, nothing got done. Then Disney's distributor RKO Radio Pictures complained that the film was the wrong length at 64 minutes and asked Walt to cut it down, make it longer, or allow it to be released as a B-movie. Walt refused all three options and it was eventually released as an A-move, just as he had intended.

Despite the fallout of World War II, Dumbo was a huge financial success, helping to set Disney studios back on the upward slope. It was largely a critical success too and has been re-released several times over the years.

Once again, in this period Walt Disney was able to prove that hard work does lead to success, and that sometimes failure is an important part of achieving that success. Although he was deeply depressed by the fact that Pinocchio and Fantasia didn't perform as well as they should have done, he learned his lesson and went on to make a film that, although much simpler, made a huge financial profit. And that is all part of what makes Walt Disney a great man – he didn't let his mistakes stop him from striving to achieve his ultimate goals.

Chapter 9: Walt Disney and World War II

"When you're curious, you find lots of interesting things to do."

By the time that Dumbo hit the movie theaters, the United States entered World War II and the Disney studios were thrown into disarray. The animators continued to work, although largely for the war effort. However, some films were still released in the period from 1941 to 1945, albeit without any great success – even though one of those films was Bambi, which would later become one of Disney's greatest movies ever.

The war Effort

By the time that the Disney studios moved to Burbank, there were around 1,000 members of staff. However, because of the war effort, 94% of that number was engaged in making training and propaganda films for the military, as well as a number of films promoting health for the general public.

Disney studios also made a series of comedy shorts that highlighted the war effort. One particularly famous piece made was Der Fuehrer's Face, which starred Donald Duck. He has a dream in which he works on an assembly line and is forced to shout 'Heil Hitler!' at regular intervals. He eventually wakes up to realize that he has been dreaming and shouts out that he is glad he is an American citizen. As the movie ends, a tomato lands on Hitler's face. It was shown in movie theaters in 1943.

Der Fuehrer's Face was far from being the only propaganda film that Disney made for general release. Mickey Mouse, Pluto and even Bambi featured in films. The American public were going to the movies on a regular basis, as a way of keeping in touch with what was going on in the war. The Disney characters were hugely popular and proved to be a great way of keeping the American public updated.

Other short films were made to share more serious issues too. Education for Death: The Making of the Nazi was made to show how children were being brainwashed into believing whatever Hitler said.

Disney made another important contribution to the war effort in the form of insignia designed for free by Disney artists. The aim was to cheer up the men who were fighting in the war. All sorts of insignia and emblems were designed; for example, the Navy's torpedo boats had an insignia featuring a mosquito and bombing squadrons had an insignia featuring a crow from Dumbo. All in all, over 1,200 insignia designs were made during the war years. Disney himself was very supportive, perhaps because of his own memories of World War I.

Bambi

Bambi was the fifth feature-length Disney film and was based on the story by Felix Salten. It was released in 1942. In it, Bambi is a white-tailed deer whose mother is tragically killed by a deer hunter while foraging for food for her son. Devastated, Bambi is found by his father and taken home.

Some years later, Bambi is an adult and falls in love, as do his friends Thumper, a rabbit, and Flower, a skunk. Bambi's love interest is the beautiful Faline. However, the path to true love rarely runs smoothly and Bambi is forced to fight another stag who wants to win the affections of Faline. He wins, but then a forest fire threatens to finish them all off.

Production on Bambi had already begun in 1939. Disney wanted the deer to flow just like real deer and, as a result, the animators were sent to Los Angeles Zoo to study real animals. The result was beautiful, but because of the box office losses of Pinocchio and Fantasia, Walt was forced to cut a few minutes off the original length of Bambi to save on production costs.

Regardless of the saving on product costs, the first release of Bambi didn't make as much money as was hoped; in fact, it made a loss. This wasn't altogether surprising, however, bearing in mind that it coincided with the middle of World War II when the European market was unavailable. Bambi also had a mixed reaction from the American public. Hunters, in particular, were quick to criticize, claiming that Disney had made a movie that was an insult to sportsmen across the country.

Fortunately, the film was re-released in 1947 and, along with subsequent re-releases, has managed to make a huge profit over time. It is now regarded as a classic.

Re-issue of Snow White

Snow White was re-released in 1944, which helped to recoup some of the company's losses during the war era. Its popularity encouraged Disney to re-release its films every seven to ten years, something the studios have done ever since.

The Three Caballeros

The Three Caballeros was the last animated movie to be released by

Disney in the war period; it appeared in movie theaters in February 1945, although it had already been released in Mexico City on December 21, 1944. The movie was made to help cement relations with South America at the time and features Donald Duck opening gifts from his Latin American friends. That theme links together seven segments, all of which feature different Latin American characters. 'The three caballeros' are Donald himself, the parrot from Saludos Amigos (another Disney feature aimed at improving relations with South America and released in 1942) and a new character, Panchitos Pistoles, a pistol-toting rooster.

The reaction to the movie was very mixed. Many critics were taken aback by the experimental nature of the movie, thinking that it was more flash and special effects than it was substance. Some critics were particularly concerned about the last segment, which shows Donald Duck reacting after he has been kissed by beautiful singer Dora Luz in the previous section. He acts like a drunkard, which is perhaps what caused the most offence. It has certainly never enjoyed the same popularity as other Disney films –but then again, it was primarily aimed at a Latin American audience.

By the end of World War II, Disney Studios was not in the best place financially, but it had nevertheless held its own, thanks largely to Walt Disney's efforts to support the war effort. He could easily have sat back and waited until the war was over, but instead, he did his best to ensure that the soldiers watching Disney films and wearing Disney insignia were aware that the American public supported them. Once again, he proved that action beats inaction every time, even if the results of the action don't always lead to financial gain.

Chapter 10: Disney Animation – Post World War II to 1955

"Think, Believe, Dream, and Dare."

World War II had a negative effect on Walt Disney and the Disney studios simply because for the duration of the war, the European market was closed and that had contributed a great deal towards Disney's profits pre-World War II. In addition, most of the Disney employees were forced to work towards the war effort.

Once the studio was able to concentrate on what it did best, they had to contend with increased competition from Warner Bros. The rise of the Warner Bros character, Bugs Bunny, meant that Mickey Mouse no longer had the market share he once had, but fortunately, Donald Duck was still going strong. A few minor package films were released, which helped to keep things ticking along, but something big really needed to happen.

Towards the end of the 1940s, the market had picked up enough for the Disney studios to start working on a number of full-length feature films. The first of these, Cinderella, proved to be a huge success, one that ensured Disney's place at the top of the entertainment ladder.

Cinderella

By the time Cinderella was in Disney's plans, the studio was not in good shape, following the box office failures of films like Pinocchio, Fantasia and Bambi. It was therefore important that Cinderella did well; if it didn't, it could have marked the end of the company. It was important to keep production costs down. As a result live action reference was used, meaning that most of the film was acted out before it was animated. Styling and mannerisms were based on the original actors themselves.

The music to Cinderella was provided by Tin Pan Alley songwriters. Songs such as Bibbidi-Bobbidi-Boo became great hits and helped to make the film successful. When it was finally released in 1950, the whole movie was a resounding success and even now, over 60 years later, it is still a firm favorite. It did very well in the box office and helped Walt Disney and his company get out of the debt that they had found themselves in.

Alice in Wonderland

Alice in Wonderland was the next big film made after the Second World War. Based on Lewis Carroll's fantasy, it was never going to be an easy film to make because everyone has their own idea of how it should look. Nevertheless, Walt was determined to put his ideas into action. In fact, he had started thinking about making an animated feature film of Alice in the 1920s.

Once the war was over and he returned to his plans, he considered making a part live-action, part animated film starring Ginger Rogers, but eventually decided that he should stick to animation. After various drafts of the story, including one by Aldous Huxley, Walt was finally happy and production went ahead. Alice in Wonderland was finally released in 1951.

The initial reception was not good. British audiences criticized it for being too Americanized; others thought that it strayed too far from the book. The box office profits were not what Walt had wanted either.

However, although the film was not re-released in Walt's lifetime, it has since become considered as a classic and has been re-issued several times; most recently in 2011 to celebrate its 60th anniversary.

Peter Pan

Another huge project, Peter Pan could easily have gone the same way as Alice in Wonderland and been panned by the critics. Based on the play by J.M. Barrie, it had a complicated storyline that was much-loved by its readers and could easily have been misrepresented by Disney. In fact, it was a personal favorite of Walt's and he would have made it much sooner, in the 1930s, but he had been unable to obtain the rights. When he eventually got the rights, the Second World War meant a number of productions, including Peter Pan, had to be put on hold. Actual production then started in 1947.

When it was finally released in 1953, the critics were generally kind, although some suggested that it had very little to do with the original play. Nevertheless, it was a commercial success and became the highest grossing film in 1953. It has remained a Disney favorite over the years and the characters, particularly Tinkerbell, are still popular today.

Lady and the Tramp

The final big film in this period was Lady and the Tramp and was based on a book by Ward Greene, as well as an original idea by one of the Disney story writers who had witnessed his cocker spaniel feeling neglected following the birth of his baby. It features a cocker spaniel called Lady who lives with a wealthy family and describes her relationship with a scruffy mongrel called Tramp.

Lady and the Tramp was animated in CinemaScope, a new widescreen format, but this proved to be problematic as the release date drew near, because not all cinemas had the technology to show CinemaScope. As a result, two versions had to be made; one in CinemaScope and the other in Academy ratio. Animators had to alter characters that were too far on the edges of the screen in CinemaScope so that they could be included in Academy ratio.

As with Bambi, Walt encouraged the animators to spend a lot of time with animals, watching how they moved, so that they could translate it to the animation. It worked really well and, when Lady and the Tramp was finally released in 1955, it was a huge success – in fact, it was Disney's most profitable film since Snow White and the Seven Dwarfs. One of the scenes, in which Lady and Tramp share a piece of spaghetti, and which Walt nearly didn't include, has since become an iconic piece of animation history.

Once again, Walt Disney had proved that, by taking risks, he could deliver the goods. By 1955, the Disney studios were once again doing well and it looked as though there was no stopping the Disney bandwagon. Walt, however, had even greater plans up his sleeve.

Chapter 11: Walt Disney and the Planning of Disneyland

"Laughter is timeless. Imagination has no age. And dreams are forever."

Following World War I, in 1949, the Disney family moved to a location on Carolwood Drive in Los Angeles. He had never forgotten his love for the railroad, developed as a child in Marceline, and, when he met some friends who had their own railroad in their back garden, Walt decided that he wanted to make his own. Lillian wasn't particularly enamoured with the idea, but Walt went ahead with it anyway. The result was the Carolwood Pacific Railroad, a train system of about a half a mile long, in the Disney's' back garden. A miniature steam train that ran on the tracks was named after Lillian herself – the Lilly Belle.

Walt proved to be very good at making plans for entertainment systems and was soon planning something much larger than the Carolwood Pacific Railroad – a theme park.

Influences

Walt started to make plans for a theme park when he took his daughters, Diane and Sharon, to amusement parks when they were small. He soon came to realize that there was not much to entertain adults in such parks and he started to think of a park in which both adults and children could have fun. He also had the idea of building a miniature railroad as one of the rides. He was impressed by a park in Michigan that had such a railroad and wanted to work it into his own plans.

The Mickey Mouse Park

Another reason for wanting to build an amusement park was to entertain the fans when they came to visit Disney studios. He knew that a tour of the studios was unlikely to be a draw for many people and wanted to build some attractions to keep them happy. The park would be near the Burbank studios so that visitors could tour the studios and have fun at the park at the same time. He aimed to name it the Mickey Mouse Park, which would cover about eight acres.

Walt visited other parks in the United States and Europe for inspiration, and soon came up with a number of great ideas, which he then shared with designers. However, as the designers started to get the ideas down on paper, it quickly became clear that eight acres were nowhere near large enough for what Walt was now envisioning. He wanted space to build mountains and rivers, waterfalls and a fairy-tale castle, along with rides and a working railroad. He needed to look for other land. In time, the eight acres meant for the Mickey Mouse Park became more Disney studios.

Anaheim, California

By 1953, Walt realized that he needed to find land of about 100 acres to house his project. According to JustDisney.com, he commissioned the Stanford Research Institute to look for land outside Los Angeles, but not so far away that it wasn't easily accessible. Nor did he want to spend too much money; he knew from past experience of the dangers of over-spending.

What he eventually came up with was a 160-acre plot of land that had once been used to grow oranges. It needed to be cleared, and 15 houses needed to be moved, but it was a great location, near the Santa Ana Freeway and Harbor Boulevard. It was perfect. Now Walt just had to work out how to fund the building of Disneyland, as he had decided it would be called.

Finding the money

The construction of Disneyland was not going to be cheap, and there was no way that the studios could fund it, so Walt needed to find funding from outside investors. That proved to be more difficult than even he expected. Nothing along the lines of Disneyland had been done before and investors just couldn't be sure that the resulting amusement park was going to return their investment. As Walt himself said, "Dreams offer too little collateral." Walt realized that he would have to find another way of funding the project.

He turned to ABC and, by creating a show called Disneyland, which explained the concepts behind the park, the relatively new network agreed to fund the project. The show was a great success and the American people began to look forward to seeing Walt's ideas translated into reality.

Construction Begins

The aim was to open the park in 1955, but the construction of the park didn't begin until 1954. It seemed unlikely it would be ready for opening within just a few months. Walt, however, was determined and the fact that he knew exactly what he wanted was a great help. He planned everything down the minutest detail.

The entry to Disneyland was to be based on an old-fashioned high street from the beginning of the century. He wanted the public to be impressed from the minute they walked in, knowing that they could expect great things from the rest of the park. The main park was to be split into four separate lands. Adventure land was to focus on the jungles of Africa and Asia. Frontier land was to represent the days of the pioneers, a piece of history Walt strongly believed should be appreciated. Fantasyland was to be the land where dreams are made and was to feature a fairy-tale castle. Tomorrow land aimed to give people a glimpse into the future.

Construction wasn't without its difficulties though and Walt visited the site several times a week so that he could ensure solutions were found as quickly as possible. He was well aware that he had a great deal tied up in the project and he was determined to make it work. One such issue was that the sandy soil of the Anaheim location didn't hold water well, which meant that the waterways Walt was planning seemed an impossible dream. Fortunately, a solution was found; the bottom of the rivers was covered in hard clay and so held the water.

As the months went on, it became clear that everything was coming together and soon Disneyland staff was getting ready for the grand opening.

Chapter 12: The Opening of Disneyland and its Legacy

"The way to get started is to quit talking and begin doing."

On Sunday, July 17, 1955, Walt Disney's Disneyland dreams finally came true when the amusement park's great opening day came around, although the great American public weren't able to visit the park until the following day.

Opening Day

The guests to the opening day celebrations consisted of the media and invited guests, many of whom were celebrities. The special events organized for the day were televised; one of the anchor-men was Ronald Reagan, a personal friend of Walt's. However, things didn't go quite according to plan.

There was a plumbers' strike at the time, which meant that Walt had to choose between running toilets and water fountains. He opted for running toilets, which meant that there were hardly any water fountains working. Many people expressed disappointment in this, thinking that it was just a ploy to sell Pepsi, as one of the sponsors of the event was Pepsi. The situation was made worse by the unusually hot weather. Then there was an issue with the asphalt, which had only been laid the day before and was still so soft that ladies' high heels sunk into it.

There were more problems. Traffic delays meant that celebrities all arrived at once whereas staggered arrivals had been planned. A gas leak meant that some of the attractions in Adventure land,

Fantasyland and Frontier land had to be closed in the afternoon. Children were disappointed that they weren't able to get on rides. 28,000 people attended the opening day ceremonies, but many of those tickets were counterfeit.

As a result, the press reaction to the opening day events was disappointing. Even Walt himself could appreciate that the day had not gone well. As a sweetener, he invited many of the invitees from that day back again so that they could enjoy Disneyland as originally planned.

The next day, 50,000 people visited the park, with some waiting in line from two o'clock in the morning. Fortunately, the bad press did not put people off visiting Disneyland and, despite the problems on the Opening Day, it became an important aim for people to visit Disneyland at least once. Ten years after the Opening Day, 50 million visitors had entered the Disneyland gates, according to JustDisney.com.

Fortunately, Walt Disney lived to see his dream become a reality, even though he could not possibly have imagined the place in popular culture that Disneyland still has today. Much of that is down to Walt's attention to detail. In the first decade of Disneyland's existence, he visited the park regularly and, if he wasn't happy with anything, he would order it to be fixed immediately. He knew everything that was going on. That is a lesson to be learned by all of us. If you want something done to your own exacting standards, you need to be personally involved. Leaving it to others is not an option.

How Disneyland has changed

Even if Walt hadn't died in 1966, he would have expected Disneyland to change and develop over the years. Even before his death, something new was added every year. For example, in 1956, the Skyway, an aerial tramway opened and Tom Sawyer Island was added. In 1959, the world's first tubular steel roller coaster was added, which became a major attraction. Over the years since Disneyland opened, many rides and attractions have been added and some have been taken away – the aim of the park is to ensure that visitors have the best time possible and sometimes that means making costly changes.

Although Disneyland was initially restricted from expanding, new areas have been added to the park since 1955, including New Orleans Square, which opened in 1966, Critter County, which opened in 1972 and Mickey's Toon town, which was added in 1993. Some of the most important attractions in the park can be found in these areas.

Of course, it is not just the rides and attractions that are of interest to visitors; the live entertainment, in the form of Disney characters, fireworks, parades and street performers, is also hugely popular. Again, characters are added as new Disney films are released.

Disneyland and its Influence on the World

Disneyland didn't just have an important influence on North American culture; it had a great influence across the world. So far-reaching was its influence that Nikita Khruschev wanted to pay it a visit when he visited America in 1959. He was not able to do so because of security concerns amidst Cold War tensions. However, plenty of other famous people were allowed to pay Disneyland a visit, including the Shah of Iran, Prince Rainier of Monaco and Princess

Anne of Great Britain.

Although the Disneyland in California remains the park that most people want to visit, other Disney lands have since opened across the world, including Tokyo Disneyland, Disneyland Paris and Hong Kong Disneyland.

Of course, since Walt Disney's visionary idea of a theme park, many other theme parks have opened based on his concepts. However, Disneyland remains one of the most popular theme parks in the world, attracting millions of people every year. Although Disneyland was, to a certain extent, eclipsed by Disney World when it opened in 1971, Disneyland still has a place in many people's hearts and, because it is smaller, is more manageable for some people.

Chapter 13: Walt Disney – Film and Television Post 1955

"We keep moving forward, opening new doors, and doing new things, because we're curious and curiosity keeps leading us down new paths."

In the 1950s, although it was still an important part of Disney work, Walt Disney was starting to move away from animation. He was replacing it with live action film and television, forms of media that he found worked very well for Disney. In the early 1950s, two live action films, including Treasure Island and 20,000 Leagues under the Sea, were released and did relatively well.

In addition, television was becoming increasingly popular and, following the success of ABC's Disneyland, which helped Disney fund and promote the theme park, Walt Disney started looking at ways to use television to further Disney's fortunes.

Film

After Treasure Island and 20,000 Leagues under the Sea, Disney live-action films came thick and fast. Among the most popular were Old Yeller in 1957, Pollyanna in 1960 and The Parent Trap in 1961. Old Yeller, based around a boy and his dog, had a Luke-warm reception at the time of its release, but it soon gained popularity and is now considered a classic. It is most remembered for the tear-jerking scene in which Old Yeller dies.

Pollyanna, based on the book by Eleanor Porter, starred Hayley Mills, who was then a little-known child actress. The film didn't do all that well on release, failing to bring in the profits that Walt had expected, but it catapulted Hayley Mills to stardom and the film has since become a much-loved classic. She was immediately cast in another Disney film, The Parent Trap, in which she played the role of twins. She would go on to act in another four Disney films.

The Parent Trap, also starring Maureen O'Hara, did well because the story was sweet, but also because Hayley Mills played twins, which involved some clever photography tricks. For the time, these were a real talking point.

Animation, although it was side-lined to a certain extent, and certainly wasn't as closely regulated by Walt himself, still featured. Some major animated movies made between 1955 and Walt's death include The Lady and The Tramp, Sleeping Beauty, One Hundred and One Dalmatians and The Sword in the Stone.

Sleeping Beauty, released in 1959, did not do well at the box office; in fact, it didn't cover its costs. As a result, many Disney employees were laid off. However, although it was not re-released while Walt was still alive, it has been released many times since and is now considered a classic.

Following the disappointment of Sleeping Beauty, Disney needed a new animated film to do well; fortunately, One Hundred and One Dalmatians was one of the most popular films of 1961 and helped recoup some of the losses. The Sword in the Stone, released in 1963, was also a financial success.

There was, however, one more film to come out in Walt Disney's lifetime that was a huge success and mixed both animation and live action film. That film was Mary Poppins, a film that has gone down in history for so many reasons, and is still hugely popular today.

It took Walt Disney years to get the author of Mary Poppins, P.L. Travers, to agree to let him make the film. That journey has recently been portrayed in Saving Mr Banks, starring Tom Hanks. Once she had agreed, it was all systems go. Walt wanted the film to be a combination of both animation and live-action, because this enabled him to tell the story with an element of fantasy.

Julie Andrews was cast as Mary Poppins in her feature film debut and Dick Van Dyke, who was a popular television personality, was cast as Bert. Both proved to be great choices. Julie Andrews would go on to win an Academy Award for Best Actress. Although Dick Van Dyke's cockney accent was far away from what it should have been, he nevertheless managed to cement his position as a much-loved actor following his performance in the movie.

Mary Poppins was a huge commercial success. It was the most profitable film of 1965, beating even The Sound of Music. The soundtrack was also hugely popular. One of the few people to dislike the film was P.L. Travers herself, who hated what Walt had done to the film. Parts were changed completely and even the character of Mary Poppins herself had been changed from a morose, strict woman to a sunny, friendly one whom everyone loved. Travers would never again consider any further collaboration with Disney.

Television

In the 1950s, Walt began to appreciate the power of television, which was only just beginning as a media form. He loved the influence that

ABC's Disneyland had had and wanted to use television to develop Disney's fortunes even further. As well as Disneyland, Disney had made a TV special called One Hour in Wonderland in 1950 and a highlight of the Disneyland series featured a section dedicated to the folk hero Davy Crockett, which undoubtedly helped promote Disneyland's Frontier land. But it was time to do more.

In 1955, a new series was introduced called The Mickey Mouse Club. The Mickey Mouse Club was a variety show especially for children. It featured a newsreel, cartoons, a serial and other performances. The serials were popular because they featured everyday problems that faced teenagers and showed them how to deal with them. Of course, this usually involved advice from adults, but sometimes the children themselves were able to overcome their problems through their own common sense. The main characters were known as the Mouseketeers and started the acting careers of many famous actors.

The cartoons primarily featured Mickey Mouse, who appeared in every episode. Vintage cartoons were shown, as well as new ones, but no matter which, Walt Disney voiced Mickey Mouse in them all. He had always voiced Mickey Mouse up until 1947, but then had handed over the reins to someone else, but he felt that he should take over once again for the purposes of The Mickey Mouse Club.

The show was a great success. Although it was only televised for five years, from 1955 to 1960, in its first incarnation, it had such an effect on American culture that it returned to TV screens regularly until the 1990s. In 1977, it was re-released as The New Mickey Mouse Club and in 1989, it became The All-New Mickey Mouse Club. The All-New Mickey Mouse Club was the platform that launched the careers of actors and singers such as Ryan Gosling, Christina Aguilera, Britney Spears and Justin Timberlake.

Walt Disney yet again proved that, by constantly re-inventing himself and the Disney brand, he was able to keep Disney in the headlines. Sadly, he wasn't to have much more time left; by the 1960s, his health was failing. However, he had done more than enough to ensure that his name would be remembered for decades to come and, fortunately, he had at least one more important project up his sleeve.

Chapter 14: Walt Disney and the Planning of Disney World and EPCOT

"Somehow I can't believe that there are any heights that can't be scaled by a man who knows the secrets of making dreams come true. This special secret, it seems to me, can be summarized in four things. They are curiosity, confidence, courage, and constancy, and the greatest of all is confidence. When you believe in a thing, believe in it all the way, implicitly and unquestionable."

By the late 1950s, Walt Disney was able to see how successful Disneyland had become, but that wasn't enough for him. He decided that he wanted something even bigger and better. As a result, he announced his plans for another theme park, to be called Disney World, which would be located in Orlando, Florida. This park would include the "Magic Kingdom," the Disney World equivalent of Disneyland, as well as hotels, golf courses and EPCOT – the Experimental Prototype City/Community of Tomorrow.

The Land

Walt knew that Disney World would need plenty of space. In 1959, he therefore started looking for an appropriate location, one that was easily accessible and would therefore attract as many people as possible. He soon settled on an area near Orlando. However, he wanted to avoid too much publicity in the early stages, which could lead to land speculation. The land, which was mostly swamp, was therefore bought by dummy corporations, which meant that Disney's role in the purchase was kept quiet until 1965, when the news was somehow leaked.

Once Walt knew that the secret was out, he called a press conference and announced what he was planning to do. Sadly, he didn't live for long enough to see the plans through, but he did all he could to ensure that his wishes were followed.

Plans for the Magic Kingdom

Walt's vision for the Magic Kingdom was basically a larger, improved version of Disneyland. He wanted to create a way that employees could move around the park without being seen; in Disneyland, he had once come across a cowboy character from Frontier land in Tomorrow land and he had hated the incongruity. He therefore wanted to build the park over a series of underground tunnels, which would allow employees to get to their place of work without being seen by the visitors.

Unfortunately, Florida's high water table meant that the tunnels could not be built underground. To get around this, the tunnels were built at ground level and the park itself was built on top of this.

Like Disneyland, Walt wanted the theme park to be based around different lands. These included Main Street, Adventure land, Frontier land, Fantasyland, Tomorrow land and Liberty Square.

EPCOT

Walt's plans for EPCOT and what EPCOT eventually became weren't quite the same. What Walt envisioned was a city of the future; a city in which 20,000 people lived and tried out different concepts for city planning and organization. He planned it to be spherical in shape, with businesses at the center, schools, entertainment and other community buildings around the businesses and then living areas on the periphery. Monorails and People Movers were to be the main way that people moved around the city and automobiles were to be confined to underground tunnels so that people were able to safely go about their business above ground.

Funding initially held EPCOT up; the funders were unwilling to let Walt go ahead with EPCOT until the Magic Kingdom had been established.

Disney World after Walt's Death

After Walt died, his brother, Roy O. Disney, came out of retirement to oversee the project and ensure that Walt's wishes were met as closely as they could be. He decided that to honor Walt's contribution to the resort, it should be renamed the Walt Disney World Resort, rather than just Disney World Resort.

Roy oversaw the plans to make Disney World into a special district, which would enable it to have the powers of an incorporated city. This meant that Disney World would be free of state or county laws, with the exception of paying property taxes and elevator checks. Once this had been done, construction work was able to start. Drainage canals needed to be constructed first, then roads were put in and finally, the Magic Kingdom was built.

EPCOT was not quite so straightforward, not just because of the funding. After Walt died, the Walt Disney Company felt that it was unable to go ahead with Walt's plans for a city without his guidance. It was therefore turned into a showcase of innovations that could highlight the importance of science and technology, as well as ideas from other countries. The plans took quite some time to get right because there was so much disagreement, but eventually, the decision was made to have two themed areas; one was called Future World and the other was called World Showcase.

Future World makes up the entrance to EPCOT and features Spaceship Earth, which is the huge spherical ball that has since become the icon for EPCOT. Within Future World, there are a series of pavilions, each of which concentrate on a particular aspect of science or technology. For example, one is dedicated to space, another to the oceans and another to automotive technologies.

World Showcase is made up of eleven pavilions, each one dedicated to a particular country. Two of these pavilions have been added since EPCOT's opening. Each pavilion showcases the best of that particular country, including buildings, shops, restaurants, themed rides and shows. To add to the authenticity, the employees in each pavilion are, as far as possible, from that country. It is often referred to as a permanent World Fair.

The Magic Kingdom was eventually opened in 1971, but it was to be several more years before EPCOT was opened in 1982. Of course, the Disney World we know today was to develop even further than the Magic Kingdom and EPCOT. Disney's Hollywood Studios and Disney's Animal Kingdom were later added in 1989 and 1998 respectively. Hollywood Studios is also made up of areas and includes Pixar Place. Disney's Animal Kingdom is the largest single Disney theme park in the world and is packed with animals and other attractions.

Walt Disney sadly didn't live to see the results of his plans for Disney World and may have been disappointed that EPCOT didn't quite work out the way he had planned. Nevertheless, he couldn't fail to be impressed by the resulting resort. It has made millions of people happy over the years and will no doubt continue to do so.

Chapter 15: Walt Disney's Illness and Death

"You reach a point where you don't work for money."

In 1966, it seemed that there was no stopping Walt Disney. He was busy with his plans for Disney World, a ski resort in the Sequoia National Forest and the renovation of Disneyland, as well as a number of other entertainment projects, including The Jungle Book, The Happiest Millionaire and Winnie the Pooh and the Blustery Day. He wouldn't get to see any of these plans turned into reality, however, because fate was conspiring against him.

The Diagnosis

For many years, Walt Disney had suffered from neck pain following an injury sustained while playing polo. He frequently turned to drink as a way of numbing the pain. However, he had decided to go ahead with an operation which should be able to solve the issue. He went into hospital at the beginning of November to have some pre-operative X-rays done, which led to the doctors finding a tumor in his left lung. His lifelong habit of smoking had finally caught up with him.

Further tests showed that the tumor was malignant and that the cancer had spread throughout the entire lung. He had the lung removed. Initially, Walt's prognosis was for six months to two years, even though the lung had been removed. He had several sessions of cobalt therapy and then returned home with Lillian.

Walt Disney's Death

At the end of November, he collapsed at home and had to be revived by the Fire Deártment. He was then taken into hospital which was opposite the Disney studios, where he spent his 66th birthday. He was clearly very ill, but still very alert. His brother, Roy, came to visit him in hospital and listened to his plans for Disney World and EPCOT. Roy ordered the lights of the Disney studios to stay on at all times so that Walt, when propped up in bed, could see the studios.

Walt Disney died on Thursday, December 15, 1966, at around 9.30 in the morning. The cause of death was announced to be acute circulatory collapse which led to cardiac arrest. His friends, family and many people across the world were shocked by the speed of his death, but for Walt, it was perhaps the best way to go. Almost up to the end, he was lucid and sharp and that is probably how he would have wanted to be remembered.

Funeral

Walt Disney hated funerals and very rarely attended any. He didn't really want one himself because he preferred people to remember him alive. However, there was a small funeral held on December 16, 1966, which was attended by close relatives only. He was then cremated. There were rumors that he had been cryogenically frozen and that his body had been hidden under the Pirates of Caribbean ride at Disneyland; the source of the rumor may have been a Disney employee with a strange sense of humor. In any case, cryogenic freezing of humans did not begin until after Walt's death.

Reaction to Walt's Death

People were obviously very shocked to hear of Walt's death. J Edgar Hoover sent a letter of condolence to Lillian Disney, as did President

Lyndon B. Johnson, who had presented Disney with the Presidential Medal of Freedom.

Following Walt's death, Roy Disney had to come out of retirement to ensure that Walt's plans for the future were carried out. As he said at the time:

"We will continue to operate Walt's company in the way that he had established and guided it. All of the plans for the future that Walt had begun will continue to move ahead."

With perhaps the exception of EPCOT, the plans for which had to be rethought following Walt's death, Roy did, indeed, make sure that Walt's plans for the future were taken forward. He waited until Disney World had opened before retiring. He died just two months later. Roy, probably the sibling who was closest to Walt, loved and supported him right to his own death.

Apart from Roy, the Disney family kept very quiet after Walt's death. In fact, Lillian and Walt's two daughters, Diane and Sharon, led very private lives and only spoke about Walt when absolutely necessary. For example, following the publishing of a Walt Disney biography in 1993, which claimed Disney had served as an informer for the Federal Bureau of Investigation, both Lillian and Diane came forward to refute the allegations. Diane was reported in the New York Times as saying:

"I consider this book – which ironically veers more into fantasy than my father's work ever did – to represent a character assassination of a great man who brought joy to people around the world."

Whatever the truth of the matter, Walt Disney has remained a much loved American folk hero. His family clearly loved him dearly, but so do millions of people around the world, many of whom were not born until long after Walt's death, but who still have the opportunity to enjoy the fruits of his labors.

Chapter 16: The Opening of Walt Disney World Resort

"Laughter is America's most important export."

Walt Disney's dreams didn't stop with his death. Although he died before construction began on Disney World, he fortunately had plenty of people, including his brother Roy O. Disney, who were willing to put his plans into action. Construction of the first phase of the resort, the Magic Kingdom, began in 1967.

Unlike the construction of Disneyland, which was completed in just one year, Disney World took much longer and was finally ready to open to the public in 1971. At the same time, the Palm and Magnolia Golf Courses, Disney's Contemporary Resort, Disney's Polynesian Resort and Disney's Fort Wilderness Resort and Campground were ready to open.

The Opening Ceremony

The opening of Walt Disney World took place on Friday, October 1, 1971. The Disney team had learned from the disastrous opening day for Disneyland and put strategies into place to ensure that the same thing didn't happen again. They waited until October deliberately, because they thought there would be fewer visitors that way and that the temperatures, which had been so high for the Disneyland opening, would be more manageable. There were approximately 10,000 visitors on that first day, but that was much less than the Florida Highway Patrol had thought – they issued a statement suggesting that nearer 300,000 people would try to get to the Magic Kingdom on its first day in business.

Another way of avoiding problems was to leave the official opening and dedication to a grand opening celebration that took place later in October, over three days starting on October 23, 1971. By that time, the resort planners could be sure that any problems had already been ironed out – there was no chance of ladies' high heels getting stuck in asphalt that hadn't yet had time to dry, for example! That was the period that many of the celebrities rocked up to take part in the opening festivities. These included Bob Hope, Julie Andrews and Rock Hudson.

Roy O. Disney, his family and Walt's family met in front of the Magic Kingdom's Cinderella Castle to give the formal dedication ceremony. The speech he gave included the following words:

"Walt Disney World is a tribute to the philosophy and life of Walter Elias Disney…and to the talents, the dedication, and the loyalty of the entire Disney organization that made Walt Disney's dream come true. May Walt Disney World bring Joy and Inspiration and New Knowledge to all who come to this happy place… a Magic Kingdom where the young at heart of all ages can laugh and play and learn — together."

By the end of October 1971, total visitors to Walt Disney World numbered around 400,000. It was clear that it was going to be a huge success and today, it still is.

The Opening of the EPCOT Center

By the time the EPCOT Center opened in 1982, Roy O. Disney had been dead for over ten years. EPCOT was the only part of the Walt Disney Resort that didn't really reflect Walt Disney's plans – he had originally intended it to be a kind of prototype city, inhabited by around 20,000 people, which could serve as a blueprint for the cities of the future. His successors didn't think that they could carry the plan through and rethought the whole idea.

It became a park that reflected the world of the future in the form of science and technology innovations. It also included an area called World Showcase, which showcased different cultures from around the world.

The official opening of the EPCOT Center was organized to take place on October 1, 1982. According to Allears.net, the preparation for the ceremony began four years in advance so that the resort organizers could ensure that every single detail was thought through thoroughly. At the time, the cost of a one-day ticket was $15 for an adult, $14 for a junior, and $12 for a child.

The ceremony involved marching bands and dancers performed to a song called "We've Just Begun to Dream," which was especially written for the opening ceremony. That was followed by the release of 15,000 balloons and 1,000 pigeons. Only selected guests were invited to attend the ceremony, which included the Chairman and CEO of Walt Disney Productions, Cardon Walker, who read the dedication plaque. The governor of Florida, Bob Graham, and the President of AT&T, William Ellinghouse, gave speeches.

This opening ceremony wasn't the only celebration to mark the opening of the EPCOT Center. Later on in the month, there were yet more festivities. From October 22 to October 24, invited guests attended a series of events. This culminated with the Grand Opening Dedication Ceremonies on October 24. Trumpeters, drummers and a marching band provided the aural entertainment. Guests included Disney executives, Walt's widow, and corporate executives and political figures from both the United States and farther afield.

The highlight of the ceremony was called the International Ceremony of the Waters, which was inspired by a similar event that had taken place at Disneyland. People from all over the world took a vessel of water and poured it into what was known as the CommuniCore fountain. The water was gathered from the lakes, rivers and oceans of 23 different countries and was supposed to represent international understanding and cooperation. Water was even gathered from the Yangtze River in China.

Although Lillian Disney was present at the ceremony, she did not speak – she was a shy woman who did not enjoy public speaking. However, as a tribute to her husband's memory, she wanted to attend and was mentioned in Cardon Walker's speech.

Although Walt Disney was long dead by the time the EPCOT Center opened, he would have been proud to see that, even though it didn't follow his original plans, it was a huge success. Not even his death could stop his plans.

Chapter 17: Walt Disney's Contribution to Art Education

"The more you like yourself, the less you are like anyone else, which makes you unique."

As well as the obvious legacies that Walt Disney left behind, such as Disneyland, Walt Disney World and all the films, animations and TV series, there is another legacy that is less well-known. Nevertheless it is an important one. It involves his interest in, and financial contribution towards, the California Institute of the Arts.

Walt Disney's plans for CalArts

Walt Disney began to develop plans for a school for the performing arts in 1960. His own strong interest in the arts encouraged him to envision a new school that would bring together different creative disciplines, including visual and performing arts. It was to be the first degree-granting institution in the United States that offered education in all the arts.

Walt's idea was that, by letting students have access to disciplines other than their own, they would be able to collaborate and, as a result, grow in knowledge and understanding. He based this idea on the work he did for Fantasia, which involved artists, dancers, composers and animators coming together. Although Fantasia was not the box office hit that he had planned, there was little doubt that the cross-referencing of different disciplines added to the quality of the final product.

The Merger of Two Institutions

The basis of the school began for real in 1961 when Walt and his brother Roy helped to oversee the merger of two institutes, the Los Angeles Conservatory of Music and the Chouinard Art Institute. One of Walt's strengths was that he never forgot his friends. His relationship with the founder of the Chouinard Art Institute, Nelbert Chouinard, went back to 1929 when Nelbert agreed to help train some of his animators, even though he couldn't afford to pay her at the time. He continued to show an interest in the Chouinard Art Institute after that and was concerned because Madame Chouinard was terminally ill. Both institutes were in financial difficulties, so Walt stepped in at just the right time.

In 1964, Walt introduced the concept of the California Institute of the Arts at the Hollywood premiere of Mary Poppins. It would, however, be a few more years before CalArts, as it was called, was able to accept students.

CalArts Following Walt's Death

Walt's death in 1966 fortunately didn't hamper the plans for CalArts; the Disney family and other benefactors all supported his plans and helped to bring them to fruition. The fact that one quarter of Walt's estate was given to the institute helped ensure that there was enough money to build a new campus.

However, the process wasn't without its problems. The first students were welcomed in 1969, but at that point, the new campus still wasn't ready. The campus was moved to Valencia, just outside Los Angeles, but because of a number of issues, the students couldn't study there. Heavy rains, labor strikes and an earthquake in 1971 hampered the building of the campus, which was built around a 500,000 square-foot building on five levels. For that reason, the students started their time at CalArts in a building that was a former Catholic girls' school in Burbank, California.

Fortunately, by the fall semester of 1971, the new campus in Valencia was ready and more than 650 students were welcomed through the doors.

Teachers at CalArts

According to the CalArts website, the president and provost of the institute invited a number of iconic artists and performers to teach at CalArts. These included artists Allan Kaprow, John Baldessari and Nam June Palk, sitar master Ravi Shankar, choreographer Bella Lewitzky, composer Mel Powell, experimental filmmaker Pat O'Neill and the animation artist Jules Engel.

The degree courses offered at CalArts include puppetry, music, art, dance, film, animation, theater and writing.

The Disney family's Contribution to CalArts

Lillian Disney was very supportive of her husband's decision to help establish CalArts. Later on, in 1993, she provided the funding needed to remodel the campus theater. In the process, it was renamed the Walt Disney Modular Theater as a tribute to Walt's memory. A modular theater is based on an idea by Antonin Artaud, who believed that a theater should be reconfigured for each play or performance. The floor and walls were designed so that they could easily be reconfigured according to need, aided by pneumatic pistons. Walt's daughter, Sharon, also made an important contribution to CalArts. When she died in 1993, she left $11 million to CalArts, which used the money to fund the Sharon Disney Lund School of Dance.

CalArts Today

CalArts today is still going from strength to strength. Its alumni can be found all over the world and its contribution to the world of arts is second to none. Once again, Walt Disney's forward thinking started something that has benefited hundreds of people over the years and will continue to do so for years yet to come.

Chapter 18: Walt Disney's Ultimate Legacy

"What ever you do, do it well. Do it so well that when people see you do it they will want to come back and see you do it again and they will want to bring others and show them how well you do what you do."

Walt Disney was an incredible man who managed to translate most of the ideas in his head into reality. His legacy is far more than his obvious contributions to society, in the form of animation, movies and television and theme parks. His productivity and forward thinking during his lifetime can serve as life lessons to all of us in the following ways:

Imagination

Imagination is a powerful concept; in many ways, it is a form of hope. Without hope and imagination, our lives would be very boring and would quite possibly lead to us giving up on life because we cannot ever believe it will get any better. Walt used his imagination to do great things – things that many others hadn't even considered.

Through Walt Disney's work, he has taught us that imagination is a wonderful thing. That doesn't mean that we should spend all our time imagining a better life, however; it is necessary to translate imagination into reality at some point. That is one thing that Walt did so well; he thought of an idea using his very active imagination, but he didn't wait for very long before he started setting it into action.

Optimism

Walt Disney also taught us of the importance of optimism. There were many times in his life that he struggled, not just in the early days of his career, but at numerous times thereafter. He had to give up on his first business because he couldn't afford it and he was hugely disappointed when Fantasia and Pinocchio did so badly in the box office during World War II.

However, Walt Disney would never let himself think about his failures for very long. He would quickly get on with other projects, knowing that eventually, he would be successful again. His brother, Roy, often worried about the financial status of the company, but Walt knew, deep down, that things would be fine. He didn't let failure stand in the way of his ultimate dream, but instead, learned from his mistakes to ensure that they didn't happen again.

Creativity

Walt Disney was creative in ways that most of us can't even imagine. However, we are all creative in our own ways – sometimes it is just a matter of finding out what our strengths are. Walt Disney encouraged creativity in so many ways, whether it was an employee trained in the skills of animation, the small child encouraged to draw pictures of her favorite Disney characters, or the student about to study at CalArts. It is only by being creative that we can achieve our goals.

Courage

There is no doubt that Walt Disney was a very brave man. He took many risks during his lifetime, not all of which were successful. Many of us take risks when young because we aren't aware of the dangers that we could face, but as we grow older, we become less courageous because we know how much we could lose.

Walt, however, never lost his courage. He knew exactly how much he had to lose – the entire world he had built for himself – but he wanted to fight on regardless. Without that fighting spirit, none of the tangible legacies that Walt left behind would be in existence today.

Innovation

Walt Disney was forever chasing innovation. The most obvious example of this is in his plans for EPCOT, which he wanted to be a city of the future – a blueprint for city planning across the United States. That plan unfortunately didn't come to fruition, but the concept behind it shows how keen Walt was on new science and technology. The desire to be innovative was also seen in his desire to try new technologies in animation and filmmaking. He wanted to be the best of the best and the only way to do that was to try new things.

We often fear innovation because we don't like things that are new and that potentially disrupt our routine. However, it is only by accepting change into our lives that we can move with the times. No man is an island, after all, and it is very difficult to live a life that doesn't involve any innovation. We could all do with taking a leaf out of Walt Disney's book and embracing innovation more often.

Turning Dreams into Reality

Walt taught us that it is possible to turn dreams into reality, even when those dreams seem incredibly far-fetched. We may not have the dreams that Walt did – few of us want to build a magical theme park, for example – but there are still plenty of dreams that we neglect to follow. There is always a reason – it's the wrong time, the family wouldn't like it, or just good old-fashioned fear of failure. Walt Disney didn't let anything get in the way of following his dreams.

He simply went ahead and followed them. There were very few of his dreams that didn't reach fruition, if not in his lifetime, then within a few years of his death. We should follow his lead by forging ahead with our dreams, without constantly making excuses for why we can't do so.

Importance of Family

Despite everything he achieved during his lifetime, Walt Disney realized the importance of family and did everything in his power to make sure his family members were cared for. He involved his wife in all the decisions he made, even though she didn't always agree with him. His brother played a key role in the Disney Empire too. He also spent plenty of time with his daughters; Diane pointed out that Walt was always there for them when they were growing up and always attended key school events. He also spent time taking them to theme parks when they were young.

Everyone can learn from Walt's example. It is easy to become caught up in our careers, especially when trying to set up a new business. However, it is vital that we have a good work/life balance. Family should always come first, regardless. It is fine to follow our dreams, but not when they are at the expense of loved ones.

Action versus inaction

It is so easy to sit back and let life go on around us. That way we don't have to make important decisions, but we also don't have to face failure. However, by doing so, we avoid following our dreams and potentially improving our lives. On many occasions throughout his life, Walt could have just sat back and rested on his laurels. However, he never did so, even when facing financial ruin.

It is great to plan things, but it is pointless if those plans are never turned into reality. We shouldn't wait for the perfect time; that time may never come. We should get out there and do what we need to do to improve our life. Even if we fail, we will learn from our mistakes and will hopefully avoid making them a second time.

Influencing Others

It is impossible to achieve any goal without the help of others. Walt Disney knew that all too well. Everything he did involve other people. That often meant having to bring them around to his way of thinking. For example, his plans for Snow White and the Seven Dwarves were unpopular with both his wife and his brother, Roy. In fact, the project was referred to by the Hollywood industry as "Disney's Folly." Yet he managed to persuade everyone to go ahead with the project and, as we now know, Snow White and the Seven Dwarfs was one of Disney's most popular films ever.

We are all aware of the power of persuasion, but often, we let other people influence us and talk us out of our dreams, rather than putting our own points across and working out ways to achieve our goals. Most of us could do with learning from Walt by influencing others in a positive way.

Learning from Mistakes

Everyone makes mistakes at one point or another. Walt Disney certainly made plenty of them. His first business failed and, during his filmmaking career, several of his projects made a financial loss that could have brought the Disney Empire crashing down around his ears. Yet he learned from those mistakes and did his best to stop them from happening again. For example, following Pinocchio and Fantasia, both of which did badly in the box office, he decided to use much simpler strategies when making Dumbo. As a result, Dumbo helped reap back some of the profits he had lost.

It is easy to make a mistake and be so disheartened that we try to avoid the same mistakes happening again by not doing anything. However, it is far better to pick up the pieces, decide where it went wrong and learn from those lessons. Only in that way can success follow.

Follow your Heart

Walt Disney always followed his heart. When he returned from France, his father wanted him to follow a staid business career, but Walt knew that he wanted to use his creativity to forge a career as an artist. As a result, he eventually made a fantastic career for himself out of something that he loved doing. Had he followed his father's plans, the world may never have heard of Walt Disney.

We often find ourselves with careers that we don't enjoy. We may have started them because we didn't know what we wanted to do, or because someone pressured us into taking a particular direction. That doesn't mean we can't change our minds and do what we really want to do later on. Unfortunately, many of us don't, probably because we are afraid of failure, or because we have families for which we need to provide. Ultimately, that inaction can lead to great disappointment because we just don't enjoy what we do. It's important for all of us to follow our hearts, sooner rather than later, for our own personal wellbeing.

There are so many lessons to learn from the great Walt Disney; these are just a few of them. The legacy that Walt Disney has left us is never-ending.

Conclusion

"I love Mickey Mouse more than any woman I have ever known."

Walt Disney is one of the most iconic figures of the twentieth century. He did the impossible time and time again. His name is still a household one, despite the fact that he has been dead for nearly fifty years, and will remain so for a long time yet to come. Disney movies and shorts are still replayed on television on a regular basis and, of course, every young child dreams of going to Disneyland or Walt Disney World.

Yet there is so much more to the legacy that Walt Disney left behind than the tangible items. His example shows us all that it is possible to do the impossible. Sometimes that means making mistakes along the way, but as long as we learn from them and move on, he showed us that mistakes can actually make us grow stronger.

Walt's love for his family is another great example. Although he worked hard, he never neglected his family. He spent most of his working life with his brother, Roy O. Disney, at his side and his wife and daughters also enjoyed plenty of quality time with Walt, even though he must have undergone great stress at certain times in his life.

Now that you have read this book and have seen what Walt achieved through sheer hard work and determination, it is time for you to stop reading and go and translate your own dreams into reality. It won't happen overnight; it could even take years and you will probably make lots of mistakes as you go. However, if you are determined enough to succeed and are prepared to work hard enough at it, there is no reason why you shouldn't meet your goals eventually.

Finally, if you've enjoyed this book, I'd like to ask you a favor; would you be kind enough to leave a review of this book on Amazon? It would be greatly appreciated.

Made in the USA
Middletown, DE
29 June 2015